GLOBAL TRADE ORGANIZATIONS

GLOBAL TRADE ORGANIZATIONS

Holly Lynn Anderson

MASON CREST
PHILADELPHIA

Mason Crest
450 Parkway Drive, Suite D
Broomall, PA 19008
www.masoncrest.com

©2017 by Mason Crest, an imprint of National Highlights, Inc.

Printed and bound in the United States of America.

CPSIA Compliance Information: Batch #CWI2016.
For further information, contact Mason Crest at 1-866-MCP-Book.

First printing
1 3 5 7 9 8 6 4 2

Library of Congress Cataloging-in-Publication Data

on file at the Library of Congress
ISBN: 978-1-4222-3668-0 (hc)
ISBN: 978-1-4222-8123-9 (ebook)

Understanding Global Trade and Commerce series ISBN: 978-1-4222-3662-8

Table of Contents

KEY ICONS TO LOOK FOR:

Words to Understand: These words with their easy-to-understand definitions will increase the reader's understanding of the text, while building vocabulary skills.

Sidebars: This boxed material within the main text allows readers to build knowledge, gain insights, explore possibilities, and broaden their perspectives by weaving together additional information to provide realistic and holistic perspectives.

Research Projects: Readers are pointed toward areas of further inquiry connected to each chapter. Suggestions are provided for projects that encourage deeper research and analysis.

Text-Dependent Questions: These questions send the reader back to the text for more careful attention to the evidence presented there.

Series Glossary of Key Terms: This back-of-the book glossary contains terminology used throughout this series. Words found here increase the reader's ability to read and comprehend higher-level books and articles in this field.

The European Union, an association of 28 European countries that work politically and economically, originated as a zone in which the countries could trade freely. Today the EU is a global economic power, with a gross domestic product (GDP) of more than $18.5 trillion a year.

1

A Brief History of Global Trade

In 1492, Christopher Columbus set sail from Spain to navigate a sea route to Asia. There were no charts, no maps for him to follow. It would be difficult and dangerous. King Ferdinand of Spain invested a fortune in the venture. There was every possibility that the ships and crew would be lost. What would cause a ruler to invest money to send ships and men into the unknown with no guarantee of success? The answer was simple: access to goods that could not be produced at home.

Two hundred years before, the Polo brothers of Venice, Niccolò and Maffeo, along with Niccolò's son Marco, had spent twenty years in Asia. They told fantastic tales of advanced civilizations possessing great wealth. There were plants, animals, foods, and technology completely unknown to the Europeans. But the overland trip from Europe to Asia was long and difficult, across deserts and mountains and through lands ravaged by disease and warring tribes. A different route was needed to bring the treasures of the East into European hands.

In the late 1400s, Columbus promised King Ferdinand that new route. When he sailed into the islands of the Caribbean Sea, he thought that was what he had found. But the world was significantly larger than Columbus believed. He had not found Asia; instead, he had landed in what came to be known as the "New World." But his trip was not in vain because this world was also rich in valuable goods: spices, fruits, vegetables, and gold. An appetite for foreign goods soon developed across Europe.

As that appetite increased, European explorers traveled throughout the New World and Asia. It was not enough to trade for exotic goods in these faraway lands. The lands and their people had to be conquered so that the Europeans could control their valuable resources. For the next several hundred years, those lands and peoples became the property of European rulers. Access to foreign goods

 Words to Understand in This Chapter

commodity—a raw material or primary agricultural product that can be bought and sold.

exchange rate—the value of one currency for the purpose of conversion to another.

gold standard—the system by which the value of a currency is defined in terms of gold for which the currency could be exchanged.

infrastructure—the basic physical and organizational structures and facilities (such as buildings, roads, and power supplies) needed for the operation of a society or enterprise.

tariff—a tax to be paid on a particular class of imports or exports.

The voyages of Christopher Columbus and others during the "Age of Discovery" (1400–1779) were made primarily to develop new trade routes that would enable valuable goods to be brought to Europe.

became commonplace, and wealth from foreign lands paid for lavish lifestyles of the rulers. But European imperialism did not last.

By the early twentieth century, the European empires had begun to crumble. The negative aspects of imperialism, including slavery, crippling taxes, and corrupt local officials, caused the conquered peoples to crave the freedoms of self-rule. Through revolt or, in some cases, negotiation, local populations regained control of their land and resources. After hundreds of years of imperial rule, these new governments were determined to be self-sufficient.

To reduce competition from foreign interests, high taxes (called *tariffs*) were placed on imported goods. Tariffs provided operating funds for the new governments and, by raising the price of imported goods, helped encourage purchase of cheaper, locally produced products. Governments also issued subsidies for domestic products and lowered corporate taxes, with increased profits to be reinvested in developing additional jobs, supporting research, and creating advanced technology.

In addition to tariffs, other trade barriers were imposed. These included limits on the number of imported goods and restrictions on imports from some countries, favoring others. Trade barriers were seen as an excellent strategy for boosting a domestic economy. In the short term, domestic businesses reaped increased profits and governments increased their revenue. But the positive gains were only short term. The negative aspects of restricted trade soon appeared.

Over time businesses declined in efficiency, due to a lack of competition. They also saw their profits drop as substitutes for their products hit the market and consumers needed to restrict purchases of high-cost items. The long-term effect of subsidies caused an increased demand on government for public services, since higher prices reduced the amount of disposable income available to consumers. Isolationism curbed social and cultural interaction and the exchange of ideas. The twentieth century brought with it the need for change.

The Impact of World War

The Great Depression of the 1930s and the Second World War (1939-1945) had drastic impacts on economies across the globe. The world seemed smaller, more connected. Isolated economies were more vulnerable to crisis and countries devastated by war needed assistance in rebuilding. Leaders of the United States and its allies decided that a lasting peace could only be achieved through an international economic order. Unrestricted global trade, leading to economic prosperity for all, was identified as the way to bring nations together.

In July 1944, just before the end of World War II, 730 representatives from forty-four nations met in Bretton Woods, New Hampshire. The meeting was officially called the United Nations Monetary and Financial Conference, but came to be known as the Bretton Woods Conference. Three important international financial institutions were established to guide the world through the postwar years:

(1) The International Bank for Reconstruction and Development (IBRD).
(2) The Bretton Woods System, setting the *gold standard* for currency values.
(3) The International Monetary Fund (IMF).

The IBRD was authorized to provide long-term loans to countries that had sustained physical and financial damage during the war. *Infrastructure*, such as roads, bridges, and power plants, had been damaged or destroyed. These countries could not go forward without extensive construction projects and those projects would be expensive. The bank was funded by dues paid by member nations and loans were issued at interest rates lower than those available from commercial sources. IBRD, which later became part of the World Bank Group (www.worldbank.org), continued after

The 1944 Bretton Woods Agreement established a system for managing the currency exchange rate of dozens of countries by pegging their value to the price of gold. This helped to stabilize these nations' economies, enabling greater trade after World War II.

reconstruction was complete. Its mission now is to assist developing countries alleviate poverty.

The Bretton Woods System was the second institution developed during the conference. It set the standard for international currency exchange, attempting to address the problem of arbitrary *exchange rates* set by member countries. Exchange rates are the price of a nation's currency in terms of another nation's currency. Currency is not universal. The United States has the US dollar, the United Kingdom has the pound, the European Union has the euro, Canada has the Canadian dollar, China has the yuan renminbi, Japan has the yen, and so forth. The value a nation sets for its currency greatly impacts trade profits and can favor one nation at the expense of another. When a nation's currency value is high, it can make extreme profits when trading with less-developed countries that have lower currency values, inflating the price of goods imported into those countries. This can force countries with lower currency values into debt, especially when trading in required goods such as medicines.

The representatives at the Bretton Woods Conference decided the member nations should agree on a set monetary exchange rate. They believed this would stabilize profits made from trade and increase the ability of member nations to trade fairly for the goods their citizens needed or desired. The US dollar was established as the international currency because, at the time, it was linked directly to the price of gold. This was something "real," not arbitrary. The gold price, or gold standard, was fixed at $35 per ounce (28 g). The exchange rate for each nation's currency was based on the amount of gold held in reserve by each country. This standard made the US dollar the dominant currency of international trade. The gold standard remained in effect until the 1970s.

The IMF, a specialized agency of the United Nations, was the third institution established at the con-

 Did You Know?

The International Bank for Reconstruction and Development (IBRD), now a part of the World Bank, has provided more than $500 billion in loans since 1946.

ference. Its mission was to help increase global trade by making international payments easier and by improving the financial condition of its member countries, particularly assisting those with large international debt. The IMF (www.imf.org) has almost two hundred member countries and is headquartered in Washington, D.C. The IMF is funded by financial quotas paid by the member nations. Quotas are determined by how much each government can pay, based on the size of its economy. Richer countries pay more than poorer countries. Quotas also determine the voting rights in IMF decisions. Richer countries therefore have more power than poorer countries. The United States, with one of the richest economies in the world, holds about 18 percent of the quotas. This means the United States has significant power in determining how the IMF operates.

The three primary goals of the IMF are to:

1. Oversee fixed exchange rates to facilitate growth of international trade.
2. Make it easier to convert one currency to another when trading internationally.
3. Serve as emergency lender to supply loans to countries with short-term cash flow issues.

Some countries, particularly developing countries, rely heavily on imported goods while trying to encourage domestic investment and manufacturing. This can cause trade imbalances and trade deficits. The countries go into debt because they have more imports than exports. IMF loans help these countries pull themselves out of debt. IMF also gives advice to help the countries' lawmakers develop policies that can solve financial problems.

However, IMF loans come with strings attached. Interest rates on loan payments are typically high and countries must participate in IMF recovery programs. These programs typically include requirements to open the country's economy to foreign investment, convert public services from government to private control, and cut government spending. The IMF has been criticized for putting emphasis on financial concerns at the expense of social concerns. Foreign companies are accused of exploiting IMF programs. This can come in the form of setting low wages for local workers in order to raise profits, managing local natural resources inefficiently, and polluting the environment. In general, those under IMF programs are developing, transitional, or emerging-market countries. IMF critics claim loan recipient countries are already vulnerable to exploitation and social unrest and can be made more so by some IMF policies. The IMF counters this criticism by claiming that its mission is purely financial and does not include management of social programs. These programs remain completely under the control of the local governments.

GATT and the ITO

Continuing the work initiated in 1944, representatives of twenty-three countries met in Geneva, Switzerland in 1947 to reach an agreement on tariff reductions. This agreement was called the General Agreement on Tariffs and Trade (GATT). The negotiations resulted in 45,000 tariff concessions covering about $10 billion in trade. Participating countries included, among others, Australia, Canada, the United States, China, France, the United Kingdom, South Africa, Brazil, and India.

Also in 1947, the United Nations Conference on Trade and Employment was held in Cuba. Representatives of fifty countries met to establish the International Trade Organization (ITO). The ITO was intended to be a third institution, under the control of the United Nations, to complement the operations of the IMF and the IBRD while managing GATT policies. The negotiations to develop the ITO went beyond trade policy to include policies on labor and employment, investments, business practices, and *commodity* agreements.

The organization's charter was finalized in March 1948 but it had to be approved by each nation's lawmaking body. Even though the US delegation to the conference had been one of the leading supporters of the ITO, the US Congress was opposed to many of the policies not related directly to trade. In 1950, the US delegation officially dropped its efforts to win approval for the ITO in Congress. Without the support of the United States, the effort to charter the ITO was dropped by other nations and the organization was never developed. GATT policies, however, remained in effect as a stand-alone treaty.

Over the next seven years, an additional one hundred countries joined negotiations to continue refining GATT policies. These negotiations, called "rounds," addressed additional tariff reductions, antidumping rules, and other, nontariff-related trade policies. GATT policies were very effective in lowering tariffs, bringing average tariffs on industrial products down to the very low figure of 4.7 percent. The guiding principles of GATT remained the same for many years: opening and encouraging international trade to increase the availability of goods, lowering prices through increased competition, and providing stable markets for goods produced in both industrialized and developing nations. The lowering of tariffs and other GATT measures were responsible for an 8 percent growth in world trade each year during the ten years between 1950 and 1960. But the optimism generated by the success of GATT could not be sustained and the system set up after World War II began to deteriorate in the 1970s.

 ## Text-Dependent Questions

1. What is the primary reason nations impose high tariffs on imported goods?
2. What three financial institutions came out of the Bretton Woods Conference?
3. Why did the International Trade Organization (ITO) fail?

 ## Research Project

Find out what "dumping" means and how it affects global trade. Then write a report about it.

Exterior of the World Trade Organization headquarters in Geneva, Switzerland. The WTO deals with the global rules of trade, and is currently hosting new negotiations under the Doha Development Agenda.

2

The World Trade Organization

The decade of the 1970s saw drastic change affect the economies of nations around the globe. The extremely low tariffs achieved by GATT began to affect domestic production. Competition from cheap imported goods, produced in countries with low wages, created trade deficits in countries and regions with higher wages, such as the United States, Canada, the United Kingdom, and Western Europe. Factories closed and unemployment increased. Industrialized nations were hit hard with *recession* and *inflation*. These governments began trying other methods to control trade, protect domestic production, and reduce competition.

Governments increased subsidies on domestic goods, particularly agricultural products. The *subsidy* payments let producers keep prices low, despite market conditions that required higher prices. This helped domestic products compete effectively with imports. Agricultural subsidies were especially important in the United States. Lawmakers justified the agricultural subsidies as necessary for national security in order to maintain adequate domestic food supplies. This was critical as the United States shifted from a manufacturing and industrial economy to a service-based economy. As industrial exports declined, subsidies allowed domestic agricultural products to successfully compete against imports, keeping dollars at home.

The exchange rate system broke down in 1971, creating another international trade crisis. Because Americans had been using dollars to buy such large amounts of cheap for-

 Words to Understand in This Chapter

embargo—an official ban on trade or other commercial activity with a particular country.

inflation—a general increase in prices and a decline in the purchasing value of currency.

intellectual property rights—the rights given to people over the creations of their minds; the right to prevent others from using someone's creations without permission and the rights to negotiate payment for permitted use.

least-developed countries—a group of countries that have been classified by the UN as "least developed" in terms of their low gross national income, their weak human assets, and their high degree of economic vulnerability.

recession—a period of temporary economic decline during which trade and industrial activity are reduced.

subsidy—a sum of money granted by the government to assist an industry or business so the price of a commodity or service remains low or competitive.

unilateral / multilateral—unilateral involves one-sided decision making while multilateral involves many sides or groups working together.

eign goods, the United States could no longer back up the US dollar directly with gold supplies. The foreign debt far exceeded the amount of gold reserves. The US government separated the value of the dollar from gold supplies and

Did You Know?

Before 1971, the gold standard had been previously abandoned and reinstated at least three different times.

effectively ended the gold standard on which currency exchange values had been based. Once that happened, countries began printing more of their own money and determining their own exchange rates independently. This also led to trade imbalances as some currency values rose and others dropped.

At about the same time, in October 1973, oil-producing countries of the Middle East refused to export oil to the United States and most other Western countries. The oil *embargo* was in retaliation for Western support of Israel in the Yom Kippur War that year. The embargo lasted for one year. When oil exports resumed, the price almost quadrupled. This made trade imbalances even worse. It also showed the world how vulnerable developed countries could be to countries using trade policies as political weapons.

In the 1980s, US President Ronald Reagan and UK Prime Minister Margaret Thatcher initiated policies designed to give corporations total freedom without interference by governments. This free market style of government was intended to stimulate economic growth through corporate investments. Among other effects, this prompted

Roberto Azevêdo, Director-General of the World Trade Organization (WTO), speaks at a meeting in Rome. Azevêdo, a Brazilian diplomat, was elected director-general in 2013.

corporations to expand internationally to maximize profits. They moved into countries with low wages, cheap land, and untapped natural resources. This moved the world closer to a truly global economy.

But how would this global economy be managed and how could nations heavily dependent on foreign trade and investment ensure that markets remained open? GATT lacked enforcement power. Many of its policies were outdated, since it dealt only with goods, not services. And there were many inconsistencies in dealing with agriculture, textiles, and clothing (the primary exports of undeveloped and underdeveloped nations). A new organization was needed to address these issues. The GATT member countries began meetings in 1986 to develop that organization.

The World Trade Organization (WTO)

The 1986 to 1994 GATT "Uruguay Rounds" set up the World Trade Organization (WTO) as an international organization to complement GATT and serve as the primary mechanism to both encourage and manage global trade. GATT was a treaty with no enforcement power built into it. But the WTO was given the enforcement power necessary to ensure that nations adhered to their negotiated agreements. The structure of WTO made the organization responsible for maintaining and protecting the international trading system, set up under GATT, by developing and defending ground rules enshrined in law.

The WTO (www.wto.org) officially began operations on January 1, 1995 in Geneva, Switzerland. Member nations include Australia, the United States, Canada, the United Kingdom, most countries of South America, the European Union, Mexico, China, and the Russian Federation. WTO is member-driven. Its rulings, policies, and enforcement powers apply only to its member nations. But as of November 2015 WTO represented 162 members, including those countries responsible for 97 percent of world trade, so it is considered the most powerful international legislative and judicial body in the world.

The functions of the WTO are identified as:

1. Administering trade agreements.
2. Serving as a forum for trade negotiations.
3. Handling trade disputes between nations.
4. Developing trade policies.

5. Providing technical assistance and training for developing countries.

6. Engaging in cooperative efforts with other international organizations.

According to the WTO's website, the operations of the WTO are designed (1) to ensure that tariffs are kept low enough to encourage trade, (2) to review the member's trade policies and practices to ensure fair treatment for all other members, and (3) to increase trade opportunities for developing countries. WTO rules currently span over thirty thousand pages in thirty different agreements. These agreements cannot be put into place *unilaterally*. All are *multilateral* agreements and must be approved by each member's national governing body. No agreement is considered final until all members approve it.

WTO claims that approximately three-fourths of its members are developing or *least-developed countries*. The organization considers it a prime objective to increase those nations' abilities to trade internationally. The WTO's website also states that the organization is dedicated to raising living standards, reducing trade tensions, and stimulating economic growth in these developing nations, as well as encouraging compliance with environmental and health standards.

One significant improvement in WTO agreements over GATT is the inclusion of rules on trading in services, not just goods. Services encompass banking, insurance, and transportation. Also covered are rules on *intellectual prop-*

Membership in the World Trade Organization

CANADA
UNITED STATES OF AMERICA
RUSSIAN FEDERATION
CHINA
INDIA
ALGERIA
AUSTRALIA

WTO Member
Represented in WTO by the European Union
Observer state negotiating entrance to WTO
Non-member state

Source: World Trade Organization, 2016.

erty, such as ideas and creativity, copyright, patents, and trademarks. Unlike GATT, WTO has also attempted to include rules on agriculture, textiles, and clothing. However, these rules are being phased in only slowly, over time, due to delays in negotiations.

WTO's Enforcement Authority

WTO members have agreed to give the organization a great deal of power. WTO rules take precedence over individual member nations' domestic laws and regulations if those laws and regulations appear to discriminate against products produced in other member nations. WTO member countries can file a request for review of other members' laws.

When such a request is filed, the WTO organizes a panel of representatives from member countries. These representatives review the law in question against the legal framework of GATT and WTO existing agreements. If the law is found to restrict trade in conflict with the existing agreements, the WTO requires the law to be changed. If the

The Doha Round

The Doha Round was the latest round of trade negotiations initiated by the WTO. It began in November 2001 in Doha, Qatar. Its purpose was primarily to revise trade rules to improve trade in developing countries.

The Doha Round included negotiations on very controversial topics, including agricultural subsidies in developed countries, antidumping policies, revisions to customs procedures, free trade in environmental goods such as alternative energy technologies, and trade-related aspects of intellectual property rights (TRIPS). Annual meetings were held until 2008, when the negotiations broke down in disagreements between developed and major developing nations.

Negotiations resumed in 2011 and in December 2013 an encouraging step forward occurred with the adoption of the Bali Ministerial Declaration. One of the most important topics in that agreement centered on export subsidies (primarily agricultural). Initial documents drafted prior to the beginning of negotiations in 2001 called for complete elimination of all export subsidies by 2013. The final document fell far short of that goal. There were no legal commitments. Instead, the agreement stated that WTO members would recognize that all forms of export subsidies are a "highly trade distorting and protectionist form of support." Members also pledged to "exercise utmost restraint" in using any export subsidies and work toward an ultimate goal of subsidy elimination.

appropriate actions are not taken by the offending country within a specified time frame, WTO can pursue penalties. WTO penalties are rooted in granting or withdrawing market access to member nations. WTO could

 Did You Know?

Since the WTO was formed in 1995, its members have filed over five hundred enforcement claims for review.

issue a ruling that other member countries refuse to trade with the offending member, in effect, greatly reducing the profits that country could make from global trade. This is what makes the WTO so powerful.

Examples of WTO Enforcement Cases

An example of how WTO enforcement of trade agreements works is illustrated by the case involving the European Union's (EU) import restrictions on North American beef. The EU refused to import beef from North America produced with growth hormones. The United States and Canada took the case to the WTO. The WTO panel ruled that the EU did not have the right to pass laws supporting opposition to bovine growth hormone by restricting imports from North America. At the time there was no clear scientific proof that growth hormones in beef posed a threat to human health. The law was seen as a "social" statement, not an attempt to directly protect the health of EU citizens. The EU was ordered to compensate producers in the United States and Canada and overturn the law prohibiting imports of beef from North America. The EU did not take action within the specified time, leaving the law unchanged. As a penalty, the WTO allowed the United States to retaliate by imposing 100 percent tariffs on imported EU products, such as mustard, pork, truffles, and Roquefort cheese.

A similar case involves the EU ban on imports of asbestos and asbestos-containing products. In 1998, Canada, one of the world's largest producers of asbestos, requested the WTO's review of a ban on imports of asbestos and asbestos-containing products by France, a member of the EU. Brazil and the United States joined Canada on the complaint. The WTO established a panel. The representatives spent three years reviewing the scientific research regarding the health effects of asbestos and the various legal documents filed on behalf of each side in the case. In 2001, the WTO ruled against the complainants. The panel ruled that there was clear scientific evidence that asbestos caused cancer and that the EU ban was designed specifically to protect human health. In its written decision, the panel stated that, because of the scientifically established direct link between asbestos exposure and lung cancer, the ban was not arbitrary and was enacted as a human health measure not as a trade-related measure. The panel also ruled that Canadian trade profits had not been unjustly impaired and, due to the history surrounding asbestos-related health effects, Canadian asbestos producers had reason to anticipate bans on asbestos imports. The panel's report was adopted by all the parties in 2001 and the EU ban on asbestos-containing products remains in effect.

Sides of beef hang in a slaughterhouse freezer. The World Trade Organization defended the right of US and Canadian producers to sell beef to the European Union.

Criticism of the WTO

Despite its own claims that the WTO is dedicated to raising living standards, stimulating economic growth, and supporting environmental and health standards in developing nations, there are strong criticisms of the WTO. Similar to criticism raised against the IMF and the World Bank, the WTO is accused by some social activists of being run by and for the richest, most powerful nations and multination-

Protesters demonstrate against a proposed free-trade agreement called the Trans-Pacific Partnership Agreement (TPP) in February 2016.

al corporations at the expense of less-developed nations. Critics claim the WTO challenges many laws passed in less-developed nations to protect natural resources, the environment, and labor in favor of the interests of multinational corporations.

Some critics point to WTO's failure to date to enact full trade agreements related to agriculture and textiles as evidence of its domination by developed nations. Less-developed nations would greatly benefit from agreements addressing the agriculture subsidies and textile import restrictions still in place in developed nations. But agreements on these subjects are being phased in slowly, while critics claim agreements favorable to developed nations are enacted quickly.

The WTO is undeniably powerful, but it is not the only organization working to impact global trade. Beginning in the late 1940s and continuing to the present day, other international organizations began operations. Some were designed to work with a particular product or service or to stimulate growth in a particular part of the world. Some were made up of member nations while others were composed of businesses or nonprofit groups. Some organizations have a relatively narrow focus, while others are broader in scope. The next two chapters present summaries of some of these organizations.

 Text-Dependent Questions

1. How did the end of the gold standard in 1971 lead to trade imbalances?
2. What aspect of its operation gives the World Trade Organization its power?

 Research Project

Using the WTO website, research Dispute DS357, initiated in 2007 by Canada against the United States, for subsidies and other domestic support for corn and other agricultural products. Determine the nature of the complaint and whether the complaint has been resolved. Write a report on this dispute.

The International Association of Ports and Harbors is a trade association that represents seaports all over the world.

3

Sector-Specific Trade Organizations

Organizations like the World Trade Organization and the World Bank ensure that there is a proper framework of laws for international trade. However, there are many other global trade organizations that specialize in helping nations that trade in a specific economic sector or product, such as diamonds or oil.

World Federation of Diamond Bourses

The World Federation of Diamond Bourses (WFDB) was established in 1947 and currently lists thirty *bourses*, or exchanges, worldwide as members. According to its website (www.wfdb.com), the WFDB's mission is (1) to protect the interests of bourses and members, (2) to further amicable settlement, or *arbitration*, of disputes, and (3) to promote world trade and the establishment of bourses with the goal of including all diamond trade centers as members. The organization's offices are located in Antwerp, Belgium.

Members of the WFDB adhere to a common set of trading practices in rough and polished diamonds and colored stones. WFDB member traders are authorized to display the organization's trademarked logo. The WFDB also works to promote better business practices designed to address common issues in diamond mining and production, including workplace health and safety requirements, child labor restrictions, minimization of trade in so-called *conflict diamonds*, and identification of synthetic diamonds. The WFDB has established a system for auditing, monitoring, and enforcement for its members, making WFDB membership a mark of reliably high standards in diamond mining, production, and trading.

Association of Ports and Harbors

The International Association of Ports and Harbors (IAPH) was organized in 1955 and now represents 180

 Words to Understand in This Chapter

arbitration—the settling of disputes between two parties by an impartial third party.

bourses—a French word referring to an exchange, such as a stock exchange, or a selling point for goods.

conflict diamonds—diamonds mined in a war zone and sold to finance an insurgency, an invading army's efforts, or a warlord's activity, usually involving human rights abuses. Also known as "blood diamonds" or "war diamonds."

sustainable—able to be used without being completely used up or destroyed; involving methods that do not completely use up or destroy natural resources.

The World Federation of Diamond Bourses provides a common set of practices for the sale of both rough and polished diamonds and other gemstones.

ports and 140 port-related businesses in ninety countries around the world. Its member ports handle over 60 percent of the world's seaborne trade and 80 percent of the world's container ship traffic. It is the only international organization representing the port industry.

As noted on its website (www.iaphworldports.org), the IAPH's mission is (1) to promote the interest of ports worldwide through strong member relationships, (2) to engage in collaboration and information sharing to resolve common issues, (3) to advance ***sustainable*** practices, and

(4) to continually improve how ports serve the maritime industry. Current issues of interest to the IAPH include:

1. Resolving issues related to the balancing of "places of refuge" needs for ships in distress against the rights of coastal states to protect their coastlines and coastal waters from dangerous cargo.
2. Addressing the issue of overweight containers and incorrectly declared container weights that cause safety problems and infrastructure damage.
3. Participating in the World Ports Climate Initiative to develop strategies addressing power supply, carbon footprint management, and clean cargo handling issues in worldwide ports.

OPEC, the Oil Cartel

The Organization of Petroleum Exporting Countries (OPEC) was created in September 1960 with five founding members: Iran, Iraq, Kuwait, Saudi Arabia, and Venezuela. The organization was originally based in Geneva, Switzerland but later moved to Vienna, Austria. The original members have been joined by nine other nations from the Middle East, Africa, and South America.

OPEC's website (www.opec.org) specifies the organization's mission as "coordinating and unifying petroleum policies among member countries in order to secure fair and stable prices for petroleum producers; an efficient, economical and regular supply of petroleum to consuming nations; and a fair return on capital to those investing in the industry." Within ten years of its creation, OPEC had become one of the most powerful organizations in the world. At the height of worldwide energy consumption in the form of petroleum-based products, OPEC achieved a position of substantial control over crude oil pricing in world markets. In 1973, with its one-year embargo of oil

Today, thirteen countries are members of OPEC—Algeria, Angola, Ecuador, Indonesia, Iran, Iraq, Kuwait, Libya, Nigeria, Qatar, Saudi Arabia, United Arab Emirates, and Venezuela. OPEC member countries account for approximately 40 percent of global oil production and 73 percent of the world's proven oil reserves.

exports to the West and inflated pricing, OPEC showed that it was willing to use that power.

The embargo highlighted the West's dependence on petroleum products and OPEC's decision making. This led to development of energy-saving policies, research into alternative energy sources, and development of additional oil and natural gas production fields in the United States and Canada. When global oil supplies hit a peak in the 1980s, OPEC set a production ceiling with limits divided between its members. This was an effort to influence prices by controlling supply.

Since then, OPEC has had to deal with constant price fluctuations, global economic crises, military conflicts in the Middle East, and continued pressures within Western countries to move away from fossil fuels and become energy-independent. Future challenges for OPEC will include developing policies to deal with ongoing oversupply of oil, countering demands from climate change activists for a continued decline in fossil fuels use, and coming up with strategies to boost sales in Asian markets as demand for oil slows in the West.

World Intellectual Property Organization

The World Intellectual Property Organization (WIPO) is a self-funding agency of the United Nations, organized in 1967 and headquartered in Geneva. The WIPO website (www.wipo.int) points out that the organization provides a forum for intellectual property services, policy, informa-

Intellectual Property Rights and the WTO

The agreement on Trade-Related Aspects of Intellectual Property Rights (TRIPS) was negotiated at the end of the GATT Uruguay Rounds in 1994. TRIPS set minimal standards for intellectual property regulations in WTO member countries and provided for the enforcement of those regulations through the power of the WTO. Some of the provisions of TRIPS are:

- Copyright terms must extend at least fifty years, unless based on the life of the author.
- Copyright must be granted automatically, not based on formality of registrations.
- Computer programs are to be regarded as literary works under copyright law.
- Patents must be enforceable for at least twenty years.
- Industrial designs are to be protected for ten years.

Developing countries were concerned that developed countries were interpreting the agreement very narrowly. This was particularly troublesome when it came to the availability of medicines in least-developed countries. The most highly publicized issue was access to HIV/AIDS drugs in Africa. The issue was raised during the Doha Round of negotiations.

In 2003, as part of the Doha Round, the WTO issued an interpretive declaration called the Declaration on the TRIPS Agreement and Public Health. This interpretation stated that domestic patent provisions in any WTO country can be amended to allow generic pharmaceutical companies to obtain licenses to manufacture and sell medicines to least-developed counties facing 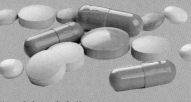 public health crises. What constituted a "health crisis" was specifically restricted to three medical categories: HIV/AIDS, malaria, and tuberculosis.

tion, and cooperation. As noted on its website, its mission is to "lead the development of a balanced and effective international intellectual property (IP) system that enables innovation and creativity for the benefit of all." The organization currently has 188 member states, including the United States, Canada, China, the European Union, and the United Kingdom.

The WIPO shapes IP rules, provides services to protect IP across borders and resolve disputes, and enhances the ability of all countries to use IP for economic, social, and cultural development. Of particular importance, the WIPO website gives individuals and businesses easy access to IP protection portals, including:

1. The International Patent System. Filing of one application on this portal gives protection in 148 countries under the Patent Cooperation Treaty (PCT).
2. The Madrid System. Filing of one application on this portal gives protection under the International Trademark System (ITS) in ninety-seven countries.

The WIPO also sponsors celebration of World Intellectual Property Day each year on April 26 to raise awareness and promote discussion of intellectual property issues across diverse economic sectors. The website includes a library of resources on IP-related laws, regulations, and treaties and provides access to case studies on various IP-related topics.

 # Text-Dependent Questions

1. Why would the IAPH monitor the weight of shipping containers?
2. Why does OPEC place production limits on its members?

 # Research Project

Research the "Bogor Goals" and find out how countries in the Asia-Pacific region are working toward achieving those goals. Write a report about these goals.

A freight train descends from the Sierra Nevada range in California, carrying a load of goods headed for Mexico. Implementation of the free-trade agreement known as NAFTA has greatly increased the amount of trade between the United States, Canada, and Mexico.

4

Trade Organizations and Trade Blocs

There are a number of international organizations that are concerned with general issues related to trade. One of the best known of these is the Organization of Economic Cooperation and Development (OECD). This organization was formed in 1948 as the Organization for European Economic Cooperation for the purpose of postwar reconstruction. There were originally eighteen European members. Canada and the United States joined in 1960 and the name was changed to OECD as the organization shifted from a European to a worldwide focus. OECD is based in Paris, France and currently has a total of thirty-four member nations.

OECD is funded by required contributions from member nations. Contributions are based on each member's economy. The United States is currently the largest contributor, providing almost 21 percent of the annual budget. OECD's budget for 2015 was 363 million euros. As noted on the organization's website (www.OECD.org), its mission is "to promote policies that will improve the economic and social well-being of people around the world."

Representatives of member nations are encouraged to meet and share experiences, and forge solutions to common problems. The organization's work addresses not only trade but economic, social, and education issues. Contacts extend beyond governments to businesses, social organizations, and nonprofit organizations. The core values of OECD are to remain objective, open, bold, pioneering, and ethical. OECD's website identifies current challenges as (1) to restore confidence in markets and economic institutions, (2) to develop a basis for sustainable future economic growth, (3) to develop environmentally friendly growth strategies, and (4) to provide skills development training for individuals of all ages.

 Words to Understand in This Chapter

customs duties—the collected income from tariff taxes based on assessed imported product values.

fair trade—a movement to help producers in developing countries get a fair price for their products, while working to reduce poverty, provide for the ethical treatment of workers and farmers, and promote environmentally sustainable operations.

halal foods—foods and food products produced according to Islamic law.

redress—to correct something that is unfair or wrong.

The logo of the Organization of Economic Cooperation and Development appears on the side of its headquarters in Berlin. The OECD has 34 member countries, and works to stimulate economic progress and world trade.

World Customs Organization (WCO)

In 1947, members of the Organization for European Economic Cooperation came up with the idea to establish a European *customs* union. In 1952, the idea became a reality with the charter of the Customs Cooperation Council (CCC). The CCC had seventeen founding members working to advance coordination of customs policies and procedures in Europe. By 1994, the organization had become worldwide and included 180 customs administrations, including countries responsible for approximately 98 percent of world trade. The name was changed to the World Customs Organization (WCO). The organization is now based in Brussels, Belgium. Current members include, among others, most South American countries, Mexico, the Russian

The US and Canadian customs stations are almost side-by-side in the tiny Vermont village of Beebe Plain. The Canadian Border Services Agency is the agency responsible for collecting duties and taxes according to the specifications of the Canadian Customs Act. Many customs offenses, such as undervaluing goods, evading payment of duties, and smuggling, are considered criminal acts under Canadian law.

Federation, the United Kingdom, China, India, Canada, and the United States.

The WCO prides itself on being the only international organization devoted specifically to customs policies and procedures and having the necessary expertise to provide technical assistance to customs administrations worldwide. The WCO is committed to stimulating the growth of legitimate international trade and combating fraudulent trade activities. The WCO website (www.wcoomd.org) specifies the organization's mission as providing "leadership, guidance, and support to customs administrators to secure and facilitate legitimate trade, realize revenues, protect society, and build capacity."

One of the WCO's primary goals is to ensure the secure, efficient, and effective collection of customs duties, and to develop anticounterfeiting and antipiracy initiatives. The WCO is also responsible for administering the WTO's Agreements on Customs Valuation, the system for placing monetary values on imported goods. These values determine the amount of customs duties applied to products, based on individual countries' tariffs.

Delegates to the WCO work together to develop modern customs standards, guidelines, and goals issued in written notices called "conventions." The organization's staff conducts research and analysis to gather data and statistics on customs and trade, working to provide what the website describes as a "knowledge-based service culture."

Consumers International (CI)

Consumers International (CI) is the only independent global voice for consumers. The organization was established in 1960 in the United Kingdom as a federation of consumer groups. CI currently has 240 members in 120 countries. The organization's goal, as listed on its website (www.consumersinternational.org), is to forge a "fair, safe, and sustainable future for all consumers in a global marketplace increasingly dominated by international corporations."

The CI is dedicated to eight basic consumer rights:

1. The right to the satisfaction of basic needs.
2. The right to safety.
3. The right to be informed.
4. The right to choose.
5. The right to be heard.
6. The right to *redress* (that is, settlement of claims).
7. The right to consumer education.
8. The right to a healthy environment.

The organization works through coordinated, targeted, multinational campaigns to both inform consumers about their rights and utilize strength-in-numbers strategies to address consumer rights issues with both governments and corporations.

International Trade Centre (ITC)

The International Trade Centre (ITC) is a joint agency of the WTO and the United Nations. As noted on its website (www.intracen.org), the organization's mission is to "foster inclusive and sustainable growth and development through trade and international business development." The organization is devoted primarily to enhancing trade in developing countries and transition economies. The ITC was established in 1964.

ITC goals include strengthening the business sectors of developing countries and transition economies and improving the performance of trade and investment support institutions for small to medium-sized enterprises. The ITC is particularly interested in developing regional projects to support economic integration on a regional level. This enables developing countries to succeed in trade within their own geographic regions and transition into higher-risk global exchange at a slower pace. Examples of recent ITC projects include (1) developing a *halal foods* certification program for food products in Egypt, providing greater trade opportunities in nearby Islamic countries, (2) improving the coconut products trade in the Caribbean to enhance the livelihood of small business owners, and (3) promoting trade in African cotton.

World Fair Trade Organization (WFTO)

The World Fair Trade Organization (WFTO) is a network of global organizations working to secure *fair trade* policies. The WFTO began in 1970 as a series of informal conferences. It was formally organized in 1979 under the name International Federation of Alternative Trade. The name changed to International Fair Trade Association in 2007 and then to the current name in 2008. The WFTO has seen significant growth over the last ten years, increasing from 159 members to almost 500, representing seventy countries. The administrative operations of the organization are based in the Netherlands.

Members include producers, marketers, exporters, importers, wholesalers, and retailers. The only requirement for membership is that an organization must be totally committed to fair trade and apply fair trade principles to its

These imported bananas bear the Fairtrade Foundation sticker. Founded in 1992, the organization promotes global trade with marginalized workers and their communities.

product supply chain. On its website (www.wfto.com), the WFTO states as its guiding principle that "trade must benefit the most vulnerable and deliver sustainable livelihoods by developing opportunities, especially for small and disadvantaged producers." The WFTO claims that the organization gives its members a united voice in global markets and establishes credibility for the fair trade claims associated with their products. It also provides training and helps its members gain market access.

In 2009, the WFTO established ten principles of fair trade that continue to underlie the organization's mission today. The principles state that fair trade must:

1. Create opportunities for economically disadvantaged producers.
2. Maintain transparency and accountability in trade.
3. Promote fair trade practices.
4. Make sure that organizations receive payment of a fair price for their products and services.
5. Ensure that products and services are produced without child labor or forced labor.
6. Foster nondiscrimination, gender equity, and women's economic empowerment and freedom of association.
7. Ensure proper working conditions.
8. Provide opportunities to enlarge or expand manufacturing facilities.
9. Promote fair trade opportunities.
10. Ensure respect for the environment.

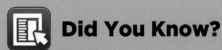 **Did You Know?**

Fair Trade USA, a nonprofit organization that certifies products against standards for sustainability and worker safety, opened its headquarters in the United States in 1998 and now partners with eight hundred companies that produce more than $1.5 billion worth of Fair Trade–certified products each year.

International Trade Blocs

A trade bloc is created when the governments of several different countries agree to reduce or eliminate all tariffs and other barriers to trade between the members of the bloc. Trade blocs are often created to facilitate regional trade between neighboring countries.

One well-known trade bloc was created in 1993, when the Mexican, Canadian, and US governments signed the North American Free Trade Agreement (NAFTA). This agreement removed many fees and restrictions on imports and exports, allowing goods and services to be traded freely among the three member countries. It also provided opportunities for foreign companies to invest in these countries, by making it less expensive for them to operate facilities there.

Some people have criticized NAFTA, noting that more than 700,000 American manufacturing jobs have been lost to Mexico, where the cost of operating factories is much cheaper. However, others praise the agreement, noting that US trade with Canada and Mexico has increased from $337 million in 1993 to over $1.5 trillion in 2015. Since the creation of NAFTA, the United States has signed free-trade agreements with countries like Israel, Australia, and Colombia, as well as a pact with a number of Central American nations and the Dominican Republic known as DR-CAFTA. Canada has signed free-trade agreements with Korea, Honduras, Jordan, and other countries, while Mexico has made agreements with China, Japan, the European Union, and other countries.

Another well-known trade bloc is the Asia-Pacific Economic Cooperation (APEC), an organization that operates through collective and individual projects. It does not require its members to enter into any treaties or other legal-

Canadians protest in Toronto during 2014 against the proposed Trans-Pacific Partnership (TPP). This free-trade agreement included twelve Pacific Rim countries, including the United States and Canada. After seven years of negotiations, the agreement was signed in February 2016 in New Zealand.

ly binding agreements. APEC was formed in January 1989, with twelve original members, as a dialogue group. Now headquartered in Singapore, the group has twenty-one members, including Australia, New Zealand, China, Hong Kong, Japan, Thailand, Russia, Canada, and the United States. APEC members account for over 45 percent of the total world trade economy.

APEC's website (www.apec.org) identifies its goal as supporting "sustainable economic growth and prosperity in the Asia-Pacific Region." The organization prides itself on "promoting dialogue and arriving at decisions on a consen-

 ## "Free Trade" vs. "Fair Trade"

The terms "free trade" and "fair trade" are often confused. But the concepts behind the terms are very different. "Free trade" refers to agreements made between nations to reduce trade barriers and eliminate policies that produce preferences for products made from specific industries in specific countries. Free trade policies encourage open international markets without tariffs, customs duties, quotas, and subsidies. Countries negotiate free trade agreements, usually within particular geographic regions. The United States, Mexico, and Canada entered into the North American Free Trade Agreement (NAFTA) in 1993 to eliminate tariffs on goods flowing between the three countries. Another example is the Asia-Pacific Trade Agreement (APTA), signed in 1975, between Bangladesh, China, India, South Korea, Laos, Sri Lanka, and Mongolia. This agreement led to tariff reductions of close to 50 percent on over four thousand items.

Free trade is not favored by everyone. Free trade agreements have been controversial in some developed countries, including the United States and Canada. Anti–free trade activists protest tariff and government subsidy reductions, believing cheaper imports will outsell domestic products, causing loss of domestic jobs and wages.

"Fair trade" policies work to encourage a living wage and safe working conditions in developing and least-developed countries. Fair trade also encourages sustainable development and conservation of natural resources and the environment. Fair trade organizations usually work against multinational corporations in favor of independent, local tradespeople and artisans. Many work to support women-owned businesses in areas when women's rights are at issue. There are several organizations that certify fair trade goods. Consumers can look for fair trade marks on products to support the concept with their purchasing power.

sus basis, giving equal weight to the views of all members." The projects initiated by APEC members attempt to liberalize trade and investment; reduce tariffs and nontariff trade barriers; develop opportunities for small and women-owned businesses; and promote technical capacity, environmental protection, and energy security. APEC has initiated sixteen hundred projects since 2006.

 ## Text-Dependent Questions

1. What is the World Trade Organization's Agreements on Customs Valuation and how does it affect trade?
2. Why is the ITC interested in developing projects on a regional level?
3. What are the requirements for membership in the World Fair Trade Organization?

 ## Research Project

Research the WCO's "Harmonized System" and write a report on how it works.

A street vendor in Quito, Ecuador, sells "pirated," or illegally copied, movie DVDs and music CDs. The theft of intellectual property—from trade secrets to movies and music and software—is a problem that costs US and Canadian businesses billions of dollars each year, and robs the nations of jobs and lost tax revenue.

Future Challenges for Global Trade

In 1999, fifty thousand people protested a meeting of the WTO in Seattle, Washington. Those protestors included environmentalists, trade union members, and students. In a statement released later that year, Asia-Pacific Economic Cooperation (APEC) identified the absence of public support as the greatest threat to *globalization*. Global trade organizations responded primarily with public relations campaigns stressing the positive aspects of their operations. Since then, activism against globalization has increased. Nonprofit organizations have been formed to oppose globalization, identifying and publicizing the effects of multinational corporations in vulnerable developing countries. The term "fair trade" has become a household world in relation to everything from coffee and tea to clothing and handmade accessories marketed to consumers on the Internet and at their local grocery stores, implying that products traded outside fair trade systems are tainted by poverty and oppression.

But the positive and negative aspects of globalization are not that clear-cut. Global trade is a complicated subject. And as technology has continued to advance, even more issues have emerged, primarily related to theft of intellectual property and industrial espionage. Economic analysts agree that problems do exist. But they also agree that ending globalization and returning to isolationism is simply not an option. The world is too interdependent; there is no going back. The answer in an interdependent global economy is to work together to identify and address problems in an equitable manner. Trade organizations certainly have a role in that process, continuing to advance the positive aspects of globalization and assisting in developing solutions to the negative aspects.

Positive Aspects of Globalization

Economic prosperity is an indicator of human develop-

 Words to Understand in This Chapter

globalization—the tendency of business, technologies, or philosophies to spread throughout the world, or the process of making this happen.

gross domestic product (GDP)—the monetary value of all goods and services produced within a nation's geographic borders over a specified period of time; the broadest quantitative measure of a nation's total economic activity.

value chain—the full range of activities that firms and workers engage in to bring a product from its conception to its end use and beyond; this includes activities such as design, production, marketing, distribution, and support to the final consumer.

ment. It is a purely human-created phenomenon. Human beings strive to succeed, and success is most often measured by the rate of economic growth. Despite periods of fluctuation, globalization has had an overall positive impact on economic growth since the Bretton Woods Conference. Globalization has had a positive impact on the creation of wealth by private enterprise without overinterference from government, on individual freedom for investors, on technological innovation, and on the advancement of entrepreneurial talent through open competition. Its proponents credit globalization with creating a world without borders, where open markets produce economic growth, cultural understanding, and a shared sense of humanity.

World Bank statistics show that world *gross domestic product* (GDP) increased from $30.63 trillion in 1995 to $77.85 trillion in 2014. In a report titled "International Trade," published by OurWorldData.org in 2015, economists Mohamed Nagdy and Max Rosen contended that the sum of world exports as share of world GDP increased from 10 percent at the end of World War II (1945) to 60 percent in 2011. Data published by the WTO on its website show merchandise exports of organization members totaled $18 trillion in 2014 and exports of commercial services totaled $4.7 trillion. These statistics all indicate the positive impact of global trade on economic growth.

In addition, statistics also show indications of positive advancement in developing countries. The share of world exports for least-developed countries (LDCs), as reported by the WTO, rose from 0.5 percent in total trade in 1995 to

Advocates of free trade argue that globalization creates jobs and helps the economies of developing countries in places like Africa and Asia.

1.1 percent in 2014, an encouraging increase. Exports to developing countries have also shown a slow but increasing trend from 26 percent in 1995 to 39 percent in 2014. APEC published statistics on its website in 2014 indicating a 45 percent increase in per capita income for residents of the Asia-Pacific region between 1989 and 2013. This surge is credited with creating a growing middle class.

Another interesting statistic is found in the opinions of citizens themselves. In the 2014 global opinion poll taken by the Pew Research Center of the Pew Charitable Trust (www.pewresearch.org), citizens in developing countries answered "yes" to the question of whether growing trade and business ties with other countries was a "good thing." In African countries, increased trade relationships were viewed as favorable by 87 percent of those questioned. This was similar to the 86 percent of Asians in favor of increased trade relationships.

Overall, the statistics generated by the WTO, the World Bank, and the IMF indicate that globalization has had a positive impact on the world economy. However, there still remain significant criticisms aimed at these institutions and globalization as a whole. These criticisms center on the institutionalized failure to recognize that economic progress, as measured by GDP statistics, does not necessarily correlate with an upsurge in the status of public goods that directly affect the quality of life for most of the world's population.

Negative Aspects of Globalization

Adam Smith published the often-quoted book *The Wealth of Nations* in 1776. He is identified as "the father of modern economics." Smith wrote that markets worked most efficiently when there was equality between buyer and seller and neither was large enough to influence the market price. Under those conditions, all parties would receive a fair return and society would benefit from the exchange. This idea is at the heart of the continued criticism of globalization and the trade organizations most in control of its progress.

Global Exchange, a nonprofit organization based in the

Threats to Intellectual Property

Globalization has sparked issues regarding the management of intellectual property both for governments and for private businesses. Open markets create fierce competition for the knowledge and information necessary to produce and market technological goods and services.

The US government's National Counterintelligence and Security Center (NCSC) submitted a report to Congress in 2011 identifying the use of cyber tools for industrial espionage as a substantial threat. Information thefts initiated in foreign locales can occur in cyberspace with relatively low risk. The NCSC report pointed to China as the most active and persistent source of cyber theft. However, US investigators cannot confirm whether the threat originates at the private or the governmental level. The report also stated that threats from Russia and even some US allies and partners cannot be ruled out.

Changing patterns of trade and economic development could also prompt any number of growing regional powers to engage in aggressive cyber and other industrial espionage against the United States. Because cyberspace allows small-scale actors and independent hackers to have a major impact, there is virtually no region or trading partner that can be ruled out as a threat. NCSC cited the greatest interests for foreign thieves as information and communications technology, military technologies, and technological sectors, such as clean energy and pharmaceuticals.

The NCSC reported that the United States is not alone in its vulnerability. It estimated that 86 percent of large Canadian corporations had been hit and cyberattacks against the private sector in Canada had doubled between 2008 and 2010. The report also pointed out that some Western European countries believe the United States is a source of industrial espionage attacks. The report claimed that Germans view the United States and France as the primary source of economic espionage among their allies and the French view the United States and China as the leading hackers of French businesses.

US, contends that it promotes "people-centered local economies" over a "profit-centered global economy." Global Exchange (www.globalexchange.org) claims the rich and powerful exert far too much influence over global trade. The group asserts that WTO rules are written by and for multinational corporations, putting profits first and ignoring social issues. International trade organizations are accused of maintaining protection for their members while forcing other nations into difficult trade situations. Antiglobalization organizations, such as Global Exchange, believe that when economic growth and wealth become the only focus for trade, social needs are set aside. Multinational corporations move away from local and national allegiances in favor of the search for tax shelters, cheap labor, and abundant natural resources. The production of private goods takes precedence over development of public goods, such as preservation of peace, alleviation of poverty, and protection of the environment, plus improving labor conditions and promoting human rights.

Another criticism of globalization points to the ever-widening gap between the rich and the poor and the concentration of power in fewer and fewer hands. Oxfam is a global organization founded in the United Kingdom and dedicated to open international markets benefiting local producers. In January 2014, Oxfam (www.oxfam.org) published a report claiming that the eighty-five wealthiest individuals in the world have a combined wealth equal to that of the bottom 50 percent of the world's population, which measures almost 3.5 billion people. The Organization of Economic

Cooperation and Development (OECD) published a report stating that in its thirty-four member countries, the richest 10 percent of the population earns over nine times the income of the poorest 10 percent. Antiglobalization activists claim the poor in least-developed countries are exploited by multinational corporations that pay low wages, ignore labor rights issues, deplete natural resources, and pollute the environment. These social ills are often "traded" for jobs in areas where jobs are historically scarce.

Critics of the antiglobalization movement claim protestors and activists are primarily privileged young people from developed countries discontented with capitalism and working to undermine and destroy trade institutions. However, the shortcomings of globalization have been identified not only by outside activists but also by members of the institutions themselves. The *World Economic Outlook Report* for 2000, published by the IMF, noted that, despite the spectacular economic growth of the past fifty years, quality of life for a fifth of the world's population has actually declined. One of the most respected and outspoken critics of the current trends in globalization is Joseph Stiglitz.

Stiglitz was chief economist at the World Bank between 1996 and 1999. Stiglitz quickly became concerned about IMF policies, particularly those requiring reduction in government social services in order to secure funds to repay IMF loans. During the 1998 Brazil economic crisis, the IMF required cutbacks in Brazilian government services to cover payments on IMF loans. Food ration subsidies were cut in half for almost 8 million people. Stiglitz resigned from the

World Bank in protest and has since worked to advance reforms in global economic policy, winning the Nobel Prize in economics in 2001.

Working with Stiglitz, George Soros, a successful investment banker and founder of the Open Society Foundations (www.opensocietyfoundations.org), calls for strengthening international political and social policies, which he believes will counterbalance the harm caused by globalization. According to Soros, social justice cannot be maintained by free markets and requires an aggressive governmental approach to advance the needs of human beings and the environment. This is the foundation of the work to be done as global organizations move through the twenty-first century.

Combining Economic and Social Advances

Soros echoes the concerns of many experts, writing in his book, *George Soros on Globalization*, that "Globalization has made the world more interdependent and increased the damage internal problems within individual countries can cause." With this interdependence, policy and trade decisions made by individual governments lead to economic ripple effects across the globe. With deregulation of financial markets, banks, insurance companies, and investment dealers all became global. With intense borrowing and the collapse of East Asia and Latin American currencies in the 1990s, the global economic system saw bankruptcies, closed businesses, and failed investments. A general recovery and upward swing in global GDP and trade levels didn't occur until around 2005. Even now, markets are still recovering.

Soros also points to the absence of clean water, adequate nutrition, and basic health care in developing and least-developed nations as proof of what he calls "lopsided development." In his book, Soros claims that "These conditions were not necessarily caused by globalization but globalization has done little to reduce them." Soros believes that the advance of social goods cannot be created by free markets. Corresponding political processes must be created and strengthened. The financial crises seen in developing nations have likely been caused by inflow of capital from trade without creation of the proper monitoring and regulatory mechanisms.

According to Soros, needed reforms include:

1. Containing the instability of financial markets.
2. Correcting the built-in bias of the institutions that favor the developed countries that largely control them.
3. Complementing the WTO with powerful institutions devoted to social goals.
4. Improving quality of life in countries with corrupt, repressive, and/or incompetent governments.

Reforms are also needed in the processes involved in sharing knowledge between developed and developing nations. John M. Curtis, former chief economist with the Department of Foreign Affairs and International Trade of

An urban slum in Hanoi, Vietnam. According to the World Bank, more than 13 percent of Vietnam's population lives in poverty, surviving on less than $1.25 per day. Worldwide, the United Nations estimates that a quarter of the world's population—nearly 2 billion people—live in poverty. Critics of globalization argue that the current system does not do enough to address the imbalance between the rich and the poor.

Canada and now senior fellow at the International Centre for Trade and Sustainable Development, sees knowledge as the future's most important tradable asset. Curtis points out that some countries will have greater knowledge and innovation capacity than others. But future global stability depends on how successful we are at making sure everyone gets access to knowledge and innovation in a reasonable time and at a reasonable cost. And while ensuring access we must also ensure financing for innovation and creativity. Curtis sees the key as maximizing the economic self-interest of a particular country, region, or industry against the use of knowledge to improve the human condition worldwide. Distribution of knowledge and innovation is tied directly to the distribution of power.

Along with Soros, Stiglitz, and Curtis, most economic analysts agree that powerful institutions, such as the WTO and the IMF, emphasize increased economic growth and international trade advancements, as reflected in GDP, over social goods. But these institutions are not equipped to deal with social issues; that is not their mission. However, other mechanisms do exist. But historically, member countries do not give these other institutions the power they need to make a difference. An example is the International Labor Organization (ILO) (www.ilo.org), an agency of the United Nations. The ILO has the ability to impose economic sanctions against members who refuse to comply with labor standards. But there is no commitment to enforcement. The United States, for example, has only ratified 13 of 182 ILO conventions and only 2 of 8 core labor standards.

A challenge for the future is to match the idealism and

enthusiasm of those protesting organizations such as the WTO, IMF, and World Bank with education and a greater understanding of the issues. With understanding and analysis of the issues, organizations can be formed or reorganized to help developing and least-developed nations create the internal mechanisms to guide and manage their inclusion in global markets. One of the most important future issues will be management of global *value chains*.

Managing Global Value Chains

The OECD estimates that, as of 2013, 70 percent of global trade was in intermediate goods and services. The systems linking these intermediates are called global value chains (GVCs). Multinational corporations continually seek to maximize profits by locating segments of their business in areas where the necessary skills and materials are available at a competitive cost and quality. This results in different stages of production taking place around the world. It is becoming a dominant feature of world trade that design, raw materials mining, fabrication, production, marketing, and distribution services are handled in different countries and even in different regions. Export in finished goods and services is being replaced by trade in bits and pieces.

Properly managed GVCs could be the answer to creating a necessary diversification in developing economies. GVCs give developing countries an opportunity to begin to participate in global trade at lower costs and at lower risk. Economic analysts have noted that many of the past problems were caused by developing countries attempting to integrate too quickly and on too large a scale without the necessary political safeguards. The key is to come up with mechanisms through which small and medium-sized businesses can participate equally while ensuring the corresponding development of sound governing institutions that can enforce contracts, secure property rights, protect investors, and reduce corruption.

Creating the Future

Statistics showing the importance of global value chains support the idea that global interdependence through trade relationships will continue. The recent issues surrounding the distribution of power between developed, developing, and least-developed nations, as seen in the Doha Rounds negotiations and the continued protests against the WTO, the IMF, and the World Bank, reinforce the idea that processes and institutions of the past must change. Rules are human-made. Economic structures are human-made. For that reason, change is possible. The call for change has been raised, but pressure for its advancement must be ongoing.

The future challenge is to combine social policy with economic policy. Developing countries must be allowed to transition slowly, ensuring that proper political safeguards accompany trading opportunities. Developed countries must commit to ensuring that power, knowledge, and innovation are allocated responsibly. Natural resources must be managed efficiently. Labor forces must be managed fairly. The environment that supports all life must be protected. These needs can be fostered and advanced through the work of global organizations. These organizations can provide the forum where ideas will be born and debated and where all countries will have a voice. But these organizations must manage their operations so all representatives can participate equally. Global organizations, if managed effectively, can create the future.

 # Text-Dependent Questions

1. Identify two nonprofit organizations critical of the advance of globalization.
2. Joseph Stiglitz, winner of the 2001 Nobel Prize for economics and an outspoken critic of many global economic policies, was once an employee of which global organization?
3. What does George Soros believe must be created and properly managed in developing countries as a companion to global trade advancement?
4. Why are GVCs particularly important to developing and least-developed nations?

 # Research Project

Find the definition of foreign direct investment (FDI) and determine why and how FDI can be used as an indicator of globalization. Write a report spelling out your findings.

Organizations to Contact

World Trade Organization (WTO)
Centre William Rappard
Rue de Lausanne 154
CH-1211 Geneva 21
Switzerland
Phone: +41 (0)22 739-5111
Fax: +41 (0)22 731-4206
Email: enquiries@wto.org
Website: www.wto.org

International Trade Administration
US Department of Commerce
1401 Constitution Ave., NW
Washington, D.C. 20230
Phone: 1-800 USA TRAD
Website: www.trade.gov

Canada Trade Administration
3033 34 Ave., NE #32
Calgary, AB
Phone: 204-983-6000
Website: www.canada.ca/en

Department of Foreign Affairs, Trade and Development (Canada)
125 Sussex Drive
Ottawa, ON K1A 0G2
Canada
Phone: (800) 267-8376
Fax: (613) 996-9709
Website: www.international.gc.ca

Organization for Economic Co-operation and Development (OECD)
Washington Centre
2001 L Street, NW, Suite 650,
Washington, DC 20036-4922
Phone: (202) 785-6323
Fax: (202) 785-0350
E-mail: washington.contact@oecd.org
Website: http://www.oecd.org/

US Chamber of Commerce
1615 H Street, NW
Washington, DC 20062
Phone: (202) 659-6000
Fax: (202) 463-3126
Email: Americas@uschamber.com
Website: www.uschamber.com

The World Bank
1818 H Street, NW
Washington, DC 20433 USA
Phone: (202) 473-1000
Fax: (202) 477-6391
Website: www.worldbank.org

Series Glossary

barter—the official department that administers and collects the duties levied by a government on imported goods.

bond—a debt investment used by companies and national, state, or local governments to raise money to finance projects and activities. The corporation or government borrows money for a defined period of time at a variable or fixed interest rate.

credit—the ability of a customer to obtain goods or services before payment, based on the trust that payment will be made in the future.

customs—the official department that administers and collects the duties or tariffs levied by a government on imported goods.

debt—money, or something else, that is owed or due in exchange for goods or services.

demurrage—extra charges paid to a ship or aircraft owner when a specified period for loading or unloading freight has been exceeded.

distributor—a wholesaler or middleman engaged in the distribution of a category of goods, esp to retailers in a specific area.

duty—a tax on imported goods.

export—to send goods or services to another country for sale.

Federal Reserve—the central bank of the United States, which controls the amount of money circulating in the US economy and helps to set interest rates for commercial banks.

import—to bring goods or services into a country from abroad for sale.

interest—a fee that is paid in exchange for the use of money that has been borrowed, or for delaying the repayment of a debt.

stock—an ownership interest in a company. Stocks are sold by companies to raise money for their operations. The price of a successful company's stock will typically rise, which means the person who originally bought the stock can sell it and earn a profit.

tariff—a government-imposed tax that must be paid on certain imported or exported goods.

value added tax (VAT)—a type of consumption tax that is placed on a product whenever value is added at each stage of production and at final sale. VAT is often used in the European Union.

World Bank—an international financial organization, connected to the United Nations. It is the largest source of financial aid to developing countries.

Further Reading

Crayton, Lisa. *Globalization: What It Is and How It Works.*
New York: Enslow, 2016.

Gombatz, Erika. *Globalization.* San Diego: Classroom
Complete Press, 2015.

La Bella, Laura. *How Globalization Works.* New York:
Rosen Publishing Group, 2009.

Mann, Charles G. *1493 for Young People: From Columbus's
Voyage to Globalization.* New York: Triangle Square,
2016.

Reis, Ronald. *The World Trade Organization.* New York:
Chelsea House, 2009.

Timmerman, Kelsey. *Where Am I Wearing: A Global Tour
to the Countries, Factories, and People That Make Our
Clothes.* Hoboken, NJ: Wiley, 2012.

Internet Resources

www.cigionline.org.
The website of the Centre for International Governance Innovation (CIGI) includes articles on global economics and international law.

www.globalpolicy.org
The Global Policy Forum (GPF) site includes reports policy papers on a wide variety of global issues, including global economics and trade.

www.investopedia.com
This online encyclopedia includes many articles on international investment and trade.

www.trade.gov
The US International Trade Administration works to strengthen international competitiveness, promote trade and investment, and ensure compliance with fair trade laws and agreements.

www.ictsd.org
Website of the International Centre for Trade and Sustainable Development (ICTSD), an independent nonprofit organization located in Geneva.

Publisher's Note: The websites listed on this page were active at the time of publication. The publisher is not responsible for websites that have changed their address or discontinued operation since the date of publication. The publisher reviews and updates the websites each time the book is reprinted.

Index

Numbers in **bold italic** refer to captions.

About the Author

Holly Lynn Anderson is a freelance writer living in Arkansas with her two dogs, her garden, and far too many books. Educated in technical and scientific writing, her interests extend to environmental conservation, history, anthropology, and all things paranormal.

Picture Credits: Everett Collection: 9; OTTN Publishing: 25; used under license from Shutterstock, Inc.: 29, 32, 35, 37, 39, 46; 360b / Shutterstock.com: 45; Arindambanerjee / Shutterstock.com: 53; Jakub Cejpek / Shutterstock.com: 56; ChameleonsEye / Shutterstock.com: 30; Martin Good / Shutterstock.com: 18; Gilles Paire / Shutterstock.com: 60; Igor Plotnikov / Shutterstock.com: 6; Thinglass / Shutterstock.com: 50; Richard Thornton / Shutterstock.com: 42; ValeStock / Shutterstock.com: 2; United Nations photo: 12, 22, 67.